They dissolve
— like warm snow —
the wine-slaked nights.

Star-crossed to the unaware heart,
our paths of glory
cross, mingle, then fork;

and the dream we were
falls apart.

~ Candice James

Also by Candice James

Print Books
10 PAK – 3; 10 PAK – 2; 10 PAK - 1
A Potpourri of Paintings;
The Still Small Voice of Soul;
Spiritual Whispers; Atmospheres;
Blue Silence; Call of the Crow;
Imagination's Reverie; Short Shots 2;
The Depth of the Dance;
Behind the One-Way Mirror;
The Path of Loneliness
Rithimus Aeternam; The Water Poems;
Short Shots; City of Dreams;
Merging Dimensions; The 13th Cusp;
Colors of India; Purple Haze;
A Silence of Echoes; Shorelines; Ekphrasticism;
Midnight Embers; Bridges and Clouds;
Inner Heart, a Journey; A Split in the Water

FREE e-books
Abstrusion; Wonderland; Fract & Flect;
Year of Divine Madness; 60 Haiku;
Midnight Shootout; Naked Leavings
The Rising; CJ Poetry & Paintings;

www.ebooks.net/poetry/Abstrusion

https://www.everand.com/author/572119332/Candice-James

10 PAK — 4

THE LONG POEMS

by
Candice James

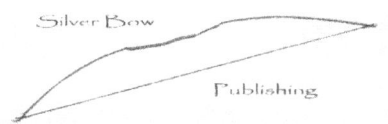

720 – 6th Street, Box # 5
New Westminster, BC
V3C 3C5 CANADA

Title: 10 PAK -4 The Long Poems
Author: Candice James
Copyright © 2025 Silver Bow Publishing
Cover Painting: "Silver Moon Down"
  painting by Candice James
Layout/Design: Candice James
ISBN: 9781774033876 (print)
ISBN: 9781774033883 (ebk)j

All rights reserved including the right to reproduce or translate this book or any portions thereof, in any form except for the use of short passages for review purposes, no part of this book may be reproduced, in part or in whole, or transmitted in any form or by any means, electronically or mechanically, including photocopying, recording, or any information or storage retrieval system without prior permission in writing from the publisher or a license from the Canadian Copyright Collective Agency (Access Copyright)
© Silver Bow Publishing 2025

Library and Archives Canada Cataloguing in Publication
Title: 10 PAK-4 : the long poems / by Candice James.
Other titles: Ten PAK-four Names: James, Candice, 1948- author. Identifiers: Canadiana (print) 20250296349 | Canadiana (ebook) 20250301342 | ISBN 9781774033876 (softcover) | ISBN 9781774033883 (Kindle) Subjects: LCGFT: Poetry. Classification: LCC PS8569.A429 A6124 2025 | DDC C811/.54—dc23

FOREWORD

This is the fourth in the 10 PAK series of long poems set out in short form and such a way as to allow the reader to rest on each page to fully digest the meaning and let their imagination run free to see the visuals and images the words are painting. This type of poetic layout gives the reader the best of experiences as they wander through the poems and travel the surreal and ethereal landscapes and mindscapes for the reader languish in and play in.

CONTENTS

BREATH / 9

INTREPID UNIVERSE / 29

MUTED ANGELS / 49

THE PIANO PLAYS ON / 69

LIVING STRING / 87

OUT-PICTURING / 99

MIRRORED DREAM / 121

PALE HAZY GHOSTS / 139

GHOSTS / 149

A SLOW FOG / 157

Author Profile / 167

BREATH

In the distance
somewhere beyond the mist
I hear the soft mew
of a lonely kitten.

As I move closer
and the mewing grows louder
I feel like it is coming
from deep inside me
as I slice through
the brambles of old sins
that scratch and bleed
the edges of my silence.

There are masks and faces
blending into one
and slowly sinking
through the wallpaper I swim in.

A flask of crystal clear spirit water
has spilled onto the dream
I am sequestered in.

I am the victim.
I am the villain.

I'm a deep red color
that clashes and crashes
the intersection of acrylics,
oils, watercolors and pastels.

And always the art wrecks
meet and collide in this affliction:
    an intricate battle
      of opposable mediums.

This is a non-painting
in the indivisible realm
of indivisible naught:

A ship without a mast.
A car without a wheel.
A heart with bludgeoned past.
A soul that cannot feel.

I am whipped with brush of color
and sliced by the knife of need.

I am the stale bled scar
on my pristine white palette
where all the colors
bleed into one
and the deep dark blacks
wax on and wax off
to a blacker shade
of eternal darkness.

But all that passes away
must come again.

All death is a rebirth
of exhaled breath
born again
in destiny's depth
of the 7th kind.

On the periphery
there are always flowers
and bluebirds
and beautiful butterflies
to acquaint the breeze
with what already is.

And what already is —
                once was.
And what once was —
                will be again.
    rising anew
in the exhalation
of a dying breath.

A square has 4 stops.
A triangle has 3 stops.
A circle has no stops,
or is simply a beginning
never ending.

Imitating life
it is infinite —
        no start —
        no finish
simply continuum.

We are the circular
universal breath called life.
We are the oval
universal breath called afterlife.

    We are unceasing.
    We are forever.

Everlasting breathless breath,
we are called Eternity.

A moment crumbles.

    A star is born.

        A galaxy smiles.

The universe dons its suicidal vest,
depresses the trigger with verve
and the big bang theory
becomes reality
again and again
in perpetuity.

Millions of time pockets pass.

Water breaks..

A baby is born.

A mother smiles.

A newborn
 takes its first breath;
then begins its journey —
toward death.

INTREPID UNIVERSE

My inspiration
rides in on a summer breeze
and dissolves in the rush
of an autumn reign.

I have witnessed
a skulking midnight moon
crash into the embrace
of a surreal noon
in an explosion of comets and stars
scarring the fiery face of the sun.

And it is enough
to give me sustenance
 to carry on
in an intrepid universe
filled with a million
risqué chances
that blossom into
a brilliance of dreams

 and sometimes

 perchance
the stuff of nightmares.

As I travel through war zones
and repo-rusted cities
I hear the bugle call a new reveille.

So I rise to march
to a brand new beat.

I speak in soliloquys
that deaf ears may hear
all my insignificant words.

I was put on this world
to say something
and now as I leave
I hope I said it well.

May its echoes
resound and reverberate
in the everlasting halls
of timeless time

        somehow,
        somewhere,
        someplace ...

and perhaps I will be there too:

        in spirit,
        in a whisper,
        in a sigh
        on the wind.

Sometimes
        I ramble on
like the annoying hum
of a beleaguered and broken
        ceiling fan.

Other times
I have little to say;
at the very least,
nothing of consequence.

But, sometimes a great idea
buried under a heap
of inconsequence
bubbles and steams
and screams
to be heard;
to be recognized

    and I awake ...

        from my deep,
        long sleep.

Slow to rise,
but alert and fully awake,
I don the scrolls and robes
　　　of imagination
as they coax my idle inspiration
out of hiding.

It rears up in a long overdue yawn
        and rides in
on a champing white steed
brandishing pages and scrolls
        of great worth;

and I am blessed with a crown
        of magnificence
in my own little inconsequential world.

The noiseless chatter in my mind
        sidles in
with a newborn vibrant voice
    that commands.

I extend my arms forward full force
hands upturned, flat and spatulate
       waiting
for the incoming alms for oblivion.

      And I wait ...
            and I wait ...
                  and I wait.

Everything is still static and stale.
all the sailboats
in the harbor of living wounds
are solemn and reverent
with sails at half-mast.

The sails are torn
and sliced and ripped
from the bloodless battles
waged, won and lost
adorned and crowned with
the ragged remnants of the souls
tossed from pillar to post
in the harbour of living wounds
and stale-bled scars.

And oh the cost.
The terrible waste
and the unforgiving cost
to the weary souls
who cannot afford the price.

They are the paupers of strife.
But alas in unwavering chase
the piper seeks his pay.

So the survivors
roll up their sleeves
and wait for the knell
of the morning bell;
then they climb the hill
to the coal mines of grief
where they'll sizzle and burn
and may never return ....

these lost souls,
these soiled spirits
who never had a chance.

Still,
        somewhere inside
        this unbreakable silence
memories drift and sway
        on a current
of unassailable fears and tears

And it is enough ...
enough to give me sustenance
and strength to carry on
putting one foot in front of the other
as I slowly try to navigate my way
            through
        and out of
            this intrepid universe.

MUTED ANGELS

Cloistered on a distant hilltop,
a throng of mute angels
mime silent songs of glory.

Unborn words
and lost blessings abound
in a stilted symphony of sorrow.

The shed tears
of benediction and love
to try to cleanse the sins
from the lost souls.

They wring their hands
and cry to the power.
The almighty power
that holds the inviolate white light.

But the darkness,
the cold, hard, relentless,
scissor-gripping darkness
pervades and parades
in arrogance and sneers —
a drunken jester
with spittle and drool
seeping from its lips.

It mumbles and stumbles
through crowded alleys
littered with lost humans.

It mingles with the mob
and rubs their pain
as it moves through them;
an infected midnight needle
filled with a dose of quicksilver joy
in fading moonlight shadows;

and then the moon shadows
turn into a rising noon
alive with sundrops and warm rain
dissolving the age-old dried blood
of battlefield scars and sutures.

Temptation abounds
all around me:
Clawing at my arms.
Clutching at my feet.

But I stand tall and resolute
      in my honor
holding tight to my resolve
    and my blessings.

I am steadfast and sure
on the line I walk.

No deviations.
No shortcuts.

I am alive and at one
in the breath of angels.
clad in the armor of prayer.

I prepare the numbness
I've become
to awaken to
the encompassing night.

I moisten the soul's skin
to hide my tears.

I become an apocalypse
of my former self.

I become cleansed
in the universal mists of time.

I watch the green leaves turn:

>	to red,
>	to orange,
>	to yellow,
>	to brown,
>	to death

falling from the heights of life
to the soils and grasses below
to mix and match into a rebirth
at nature's beckoning and mercy.

In the juxtaposition
of a small metamorphosis
and the jaws of life incarnate,
I am reborn and baptized
in the river of redemption's blood:

And it is good.
And it is just.

      And
it is my destiny to be
what the winds of change
mold me to be.

I ride the coat tails
of a fervent summer breeze
chased by an autumn hurricane
relentlessly running from
winter's icy embrace.

But there is no escape —
      no respite.

There are no doors
in this house I've built
so I hunker down
into myself and my dreams
where all is exactly
the way I want it to be.

And yes,
after all our seasons
of love and strife,
you are there
with me still.

I am an interrogatory spirit of choice
        defamed
by my errant demonstrative soul.

My heart is missing
in God's lost and found
and the key to redemption
is rusted in time's lock
and I am imprisoned in my pantomime
where ghosts and grief
square dance in circles
slipping and sliding
on a dance floor of tears.

But I believe,

Yes, I still believe
there is salvation
somewhere nearby.

And I believe
the muted angels
watching over me
will break their silence
and I will hear the songs of glory
they are singing
and they will gently take my hand
      and lead me
onto the path of salvation
I've searched for so long.

And now,
growing ever louder,

I hear the angels singing ...
          singing...
              singing me home.

THE PIANO PLAYS ON

I lean into
the wet of the 7th rain.

I sit at the dusty piano
of yesterday's echoing song
as the puzzle pieces
drop down
from the zippered pocket
of a renegade outlaw fog
and become a reverent symphony.

On a sunny, tree-lined street
    I walk alone
amongst the bird song.

Encased in a blanket
of morality's sins,
I envision childhood's dreams
lying amongst tattered photo albums
and broken toys in the attic.

Dark, darker, darkest
I fall into my lonely soul

Oh what a dastardly
      shock it is
to gaze into the mirror
   and see only air.

Where is the spirit in the body?
Where is it hiding and why?

And why is the heart
bereft of it's beat?

Why am I here
and not back there?

I'm alone with a past
I cannot repair
and a thousand ghosts
dance on the graves
that hold the bones of all my sins,
the flesh of all my sorrows,
and the stone cold story
of all my incarnations.

There's a girl and a dog
and a father and mother
resurrected in the tapestry
of all my yesterdays
weaving and re-weaving
the fabric of all my tomorrows.

I'm embellishing the good
and erasing the stain of the bad
with a swashbuckling
penultimate script
forming an invisible ink signature
editing and re-editing
my same old sordid story
in a never-ending loop
that never stumbles,
never changes.

I may be bloody
but I am not bruised.
I am just a forever wound,
opening and closing,
always in the process
of trying to heal.

I lean into the wet of the rain
as it glistens on the wind's cheek.
    I feel the cut of its lips
as it mimes the words of my song.

Yesterday's ghostly ebony piano
plays surreptitiously to accompany
the restless diminished chords
as they flee in silk slippers
trying to outrun
the wet of the rain.

Beguiling and faithless
as a cloyed 2nd hand smile
the lovers come and go
in the candlelight
in the starlight
in the streetlamp glow.

Time and again
I have turned away
from the weary autumn sun
trying to recapture the summer wind
that could turn my winter hair
and my world to gold again.

I am walking in solitude
through a troubled midnight
at odds with the tranquility
of God's eternal repose
suspended in uneven time
between heaven and hell
somewhere near where
the last angel fell.

And I think I see a wet eye.
And I think I hear a tear fall.

But it's only a dream
and I am still alive and dead
on the slick, slippery side
of the steep mountain of time.

Climbing seems impossible.
Not trying seems unconscionable.

I envision a throng
of ragged angels
and a haphazard harp
playing out of tune.

Where are the urchins?
Where are the clowns
in this cirque-de-sky circus
turned inside out and upside down?

Alas, it seems
I am the ringmaster:
A jackass of all trades
and master of none.

The juggler of time is laughing
as he tosses the puzzle pieces
of life and death
into eternity's rhythmic ,
orchestral, fiery flame.

I realize
there is nothing I can do
to enhance or detract from
the masquerade,
so I lean back into the slick
and the wet of the rain
and blend into the piano
of yesterday's song
as the piano plays on
in symphonic reverence to
the heartbeat of forever.

    AND ...

As I fade from life
the piano plays on,
        and on
                and on ,,,
                      then fades out.

LIVING STRING

I'm parked 1 ½ blocks
from our old home
on Blair Avenue
where my 8 year old self
and my mother live.

So near
                      yet so far away.

The trees and flowers
seem less colorful.
The sky more overcast.

But if I listen carefully
I can almost hear her voice.

      I swear
I can smell her perfume.

Then of a sudden,
the trees and flowers
begin to shimmer and shine
beneath a clear blue sky.

I think I am both
back in the past
here in the present
and forward in the future
and all my pending futures.

Perhaps, as science avers,
all time is happening now,
    concurrently
like prison sentences
 sliding and scraping
  over themselves.

And the pasts,
both glorious and inglorious,
are always alive
and sparring for position
in the corners of my memory
and on the streets
of my dreams.

So, even though I am here,
    in this space,
today is sandwiched between
yesterday and tomorrow
  as they slip and slide
on the mayonnaise of time.

And NOW...
I see my 12-year-old self
sitting in the kitchen
 enjoying the view
of the low rise buildings
and the ever-present
slow flowing Fraser River.

I close my eyes and call to myself
    and I whisper

"Be good to your mother."

AND

I hope the present
can influence the past
and construct another future
without annihilating the present
as it becomes the past again.

No erasures please.
Let them all vibrate
in harmony and disharmony
on the living string I am.

Out-Picturing

The feathered touch
of heaven's breath
skims the surface of my lips
in whiskey warm kisses.

I awaken to its caress.

A long overdue evolution
of thought's sound
permeating everywhere
and nowhere
in simultaneous spontaneity
paints a rainbow of song
onto my wakening senses.

Crystalline wet whispers
pitch promises and woo
to the spidery webs of stardust
creating the new trails of oblivion
that I am destined to travel.

I see you
in all your shining glory
standing in the shadow of a star
sprinkled with silver sequins
and gilded gold flakes
infusing me with sacred breath
coaxing the dream I am into life

I throw off
the coal black blanket of night,
and strike the elements aflame
calling them by name and rank
lining them up to be
what I want them to be:

My soldiers of fortune
in a land of the lost
alive with great treasures,
and sacrosanct pleasures.

Spiralling out
from a distant constellation,
now drawing closer and closer,
a purple satin river appears
and regal upon it, a sailboat
with mahogany masts
and pristine white sails
navigates its perilous way through
my harbor of tidal waves.

As the sailboat arrives at my dock,
    I see myself
standing stiff on the deck.

    I see myself
standing on the dock.
    I see myself
in faceted time lapse.
    I see myself
in reverse slow motion
      becoming...

    becoming
the boat and the dock,
    the sea and sky.

I fall into a deep sleep
for almost a million
star-drizzled years.

THEN...

Somewhere
deep inside my mind
I feel a series of sensuous chills
racing in tender torment
through my body
and soul.

My cheeks are cut
by the wind's whip.
My eyes are damp
from the sea's tears.
as they sweep the horizon
in agitated expectation
and find only a barren land.

No buildings,
no trees,
no animal sounds.

Nothing...
even less than nothing.

The white underside of night
has broken through the black.

A sweet release from the dark
            before
the night of a thousand winters
    creeps into my being.

In a world of selective absolutes
the universe becomes
a rigid metallic spinning
of languages, eyes,
souls, and beliefs.

Abstraction morphs into abstrusion.
Enlightenment turns dark.
Fire burns to red then ebony
    then fizzles out
and turns to cold grey ash.

I

I am my own path to paradise
littered with rusted out signs.

I am my own dead-end road
and there is no way out
of this dilemma of delirium.

Camouflaged
time-worn love letters,
nudge their way
into my weary memory bank
where deposits
have become a nonentity
and unexpected withdrawals
are beating on bankruptcy's door.

The ghost of yesterday's indiscretion
is birthing again and growing taller.

And regardless of how ragged
the ghost becomes,
the pale essence
of flesh and bone
    renewing
adds a new dimension
to this dimension.

An atom splits
to birth a quark and muon
Siamese twin.

Each instant is a fragment
of the past married to the present
      as it ushers in
a flamboyant fictitious future
    too high strung
   to meet expectations.

I am the impression of my intellect.
I am the essence of star seed.
I am born and I expire.
I am continuous energy
constantly renewing:
 life after death
    after life
   after death.

I am my own paintings.
I am my own music.
I am the I AM of my own universe.

   I am thought '
OUT-PICTURING' itself
   to become
 the 'I AM' I am.

Mirrored Dream

In a wet Waterworld
of burning teardrops
I saw you in a mirrored dream
I couldn't lay claim to —
no matter how hard I tried.

I can't
hold water in my palm.
I can't
bring clouds down from the sky.
I can't
turn Monday back into Sunday
And...

I can't
make you love me.

There is a mini pause
between pauses.
Like the split-second pause
between inhaling and exhaling.
Like the gap between pulse beats.

I wonder if death is just a time
when these pauses and gaps
are stretched into an infinity
we've always been aware of
 ...always been in.

Hide the moon
behind the curtain of night.
Draw back the waters
and turn the tide.

Turn the sun to ice.
Turn the stars to coal
and may this dark, dark night
cover me in cold, cold ice
until you come to me.

It's a different kind of night.
There's a different feel
to the air I breathe.

The ceiling lights and t.v.
aren't as bright
and I am somewhat
at loose ends.

I sit alone.
I have ostracized myself
from the peripheral world
of people.around me
that surround me.

I am lost in time
somewhere.

Standing in the rain
and the fallout of the clouds
in your eyes, I begin to know
the beating of your heart —
at first an echo tapping
on the backbeat of my soul
becoming a wet symphony
of dreams that drown
in the pools of your eyes
overflowing, becoming streams
then rivers then lakes.

    And I ...
I'm unable to swim
your torrent of rapids.

The railway tracks
and beach pebble-strewn paths
of my childhood seem closer to me
the farther away from them I get.

And isn't this just like life?
A circle: no beginning, no end.

The further we are from the start
the further we get from the end
        and then
        SUDDENLY
we are back at the beginning
walking the same railway tracks
and beach pebble-strewn paths ...
        and always ...
           always
we fail to recognize them.

A ring of blue light appears above
and voices ring in the air
as I sit here in my ring
of loneliness.

Images pass by in a faded parade
of yesterdays I can't quite recall.

Spring, summer, fall
are only a memory
tinged with sighs and tears
that churn and burn.
in a fade in — fade out movie
like a hungry pathetic wolf
     at the door;
   pacing, starving
but too timid to come in.

Dressed in a cold, broken twilight
I'm not one to ride the river with.

Born under a fragile waning moon
and a retrograde Mercury
my footsteps leave no traces.

My kisses leave no moisture
and my heart leaves no sound
as its beating fades away
in synch with my shadow.

I flee from a worn-out chair
to become a lost bird
on a dancefloor of dreams
that can't come true.

Roads without end.
Lights without shine.
Music without heart
and emptiness ...
emptiness all around
    everywhere —

    without you.

I'm held under the gloom
of a doomed whisper
sent out to the universe
that you might hear
the pleading in it.

It's there...
but just in an undertone
      so soft ...
    barely audible
but I believe you will hear it
      and
  you will come to me.

In a rowboat
in the middle of an ocean
with only one oar
and 500 miles from shore.

That's how I feel
this night of nights
without you in it.

There is a plane flying above
skywriting love letters
to the blue blanket overhead.

And I am sitting here
writing love poems
to the invisible man,
breathing on them
hoping to bring him to me
as I blow kisses
onto a lazy wind.

The further we are from the start
the further we get from the end
and then SUDDENLY
we are back at the beginning
walking the same railway tracks
and beach pebble strewn paths —

and always ... always

I see you in a mirrored dream
and I realize ...
you will never be mine.

Pale Hazy Ghosts

Inside the-thinning mists
pale hazy ghosts sway
to the music only they can hear —
a romantic rhythm creeps in
on little mouse feet —

    Each old song
seems newer than it was.

Now the rhythm turns gold,
tumbles, rocks, and rolls
in the sequined jazz pockets
of treble clefs and bass lines
changing moods and timbre,
as they deepen to new shades
of red, blue, and purple

A suspended chord is held hostage
in the still of a haunting silence
behind a diaphanous veil of semi-tones
gracing the ebony piano keys
in a lightning rod moment of rapture.

Life and death dance
to the end of love.
The atmosphere thickens
and trembles.

The pale hazy ghosts
relax into their smiles
as if touched by an angel
    and saved
by divine redemption.

The last remnants
of moonlight dissolve.
The lollipop autumn sun
begins to rise.

The orchestra tunes their instruments.
The conductor waves his baton
and the band strike up,

Another dance begins
with life and death,
the unwilling dancers,
in their never-ending
circle dance of fate.

Inside the-dimensional
mosaic of night —
secrets, charms,
and sacred epiphanies
whisper through the lips of dead lovers.

Their words weave sequined threads
into the liquid dreams
of a petulant sky.

The wind picks up playfully
and ruffles the river's raincoat
and sculpts the waves to crest
in goose-pimple peaks and valleys.

Nature is the ultimate artist
sometimes sketching in charcoal and snow
other times painting in acrylics,
oils, pastels, and watercolors.

The wind becomes still.
The night becomes silent.
The listeners have fallen asleep
to the music no longer playing.

A stone-shaped silence,
an indistinguishable sound,
invades neither space or time
nor thoughts or dreams.

Desert dunes disintegrate.
Pyramids crumble
and Life and Death
hold hands and hold court
in the circle game
of existence,

I am present
but undetected
and unreflected
in mirrors.

I am the mirrored reflection
of the air I hide in.

Inside the-thinning mists
I sway with pale hazy ghosts
to the music only we can hear.

Ghosts

Midnight's shine of gossamer stars
spins a web of wonder
against a pirouetting vagrant moon.
And wayward angels draw near
to feel the rush of senses and soul.

The dark-honey sky melts and fades.
Flashes of approaching daybreak
poke through night's dissolving lace.

All things pass away
then come to pass again.

A liquid blue melody creeps in
and reverberates
beyond the pale of the veil.

A rainbow bursts forth
and a poem is born;
pearls of wisdom
bathe in sorrow's joy.

When I awake late at night
I swear I hear your laughter;
and still, yes, even now
I feel the wet of your tears.

Encased in a circular universe
inside a sharp-edged square
love bled out of our being
and we became each other's death.

The harsh salt sea of regret
has no islands or shorelines.
I have survived unrequited love
I have ran betrayal's rapids

I am a dream defying death.
I am an answer opposing logic.
I am a breath of breathless air.
I am a word that cannot be written
I am a sound that cannot be spoken.
I am created but I do not exist:
I am art imitating life.

Between two binary hearts,
between two heartbeats
between the damp of kisses —
between the rush of blood
we know a small eternity.

I walk as a ghost sheltered from
    a harsh December
but still shivering in my heart
as I continue to elude
Death's bony fingers
and avoid its rattling breath
as I crack and splinter
into scattered starlight.

September became mist then snow
as it settled into winter
and changed its name
    to December.

January snuck in on snowflakes
and left quietly on a rainy night.
leaving only the disappearing frost
of damaged and lost hope.

The crescent moon
I once stood under
has waxed unexpectedly full
and now it will turn inside out
and become a new moon
without me — without me.

I will have no breath,
no body, no flesh, no bone
no blood, no form,
    but still
    I will be.

I am trapped in a prison
of blue-black agonizing dark light
without that which is meant to be,
So, I wait...
        and I wait ... and I wait.

I will walk and talk with ghosts,
peering into and passing through
the stained glass windows
of an eternity I always
return to time and again.

The winds of paradise drift in.
Our footprints in the sand
are not visible anymore,

And I wonder:
if they were ever there,
if we were ever there.
      If we were ever anything ...
          but ghosts.

A Slow Fog

A slow fog
shivers and huddles
in the library archway
awash
in midnight moonglow.

A gold-leaf, ornate door,
in lazy repose,
creaks open.

Varnished bookcases appear:
clutching antique books,
spilling forgotten words,
whispering age old secrets.

And the rainbows in my eyes
— neon, fiery pastels —
    tickle the fancy
of my sleeping dream
to awaken my sixth sense.

The runes of long ago kingdoms
prance with marauding ghosts,
whirling around each other
in magnetic binary fashion.

Stars forever destined to
come together again and again,
etching new chapters onto each other
as they write the book of *"them"*

The heavy exhalation of air
from the dusty lungs of a star,
crunches the snow of a black hole
and swoons in the arms
of lusty dark matter.

Silence becomes deafening
    as it screams
through the stringed offerings
  of a beautiful violin solo.

And I am certain we are siblings
in organic twin dimensions.

>   But
> in stark reality
> we are not twins.

Still I cling to the certainty
afraid to embrace the reality.

And
the sweet bird of youth
is tiring
and trading places with
the old grey owl ...

becoming an albatross
destined to turn into
a phoenix rising

from
a slow
familiar
fog.

AUTHOR PROFILE

Candice James is a professional poet, musician, singer, songwriter and visual artist. She was appointed Poet Laureate Emerita of New Westminster BC by order if City Council in November 2016 after serving 2 back-to-back three-year terms as Poet Laureate. She is founder of Royal City Literary Arts Society, and Fred Cogswell Award for Excellence in Poetry and past president of the Federation of BC Writers. She's a full member of the League of Canadian Poets and the author of more than 28 books of poetry through 6 Publishing Houses.

Her first book A SPLIT IN THE WATER was published in 1979 by Fiddlehead Poetry Books, University of New Brunswick CANADA. Her awards include Pandora's Collective Citizen of the Year; Bernie Legge Platinum Awards Artist of the Year.

www.ingramcontent.com/pod-product-compliance
Lightning Source LLC
Chambersburg PA
CBHW071242070526
44583CB00017B/2295